Body Beasts

PIONEER EDITION

By Peter Winkler

CONTENTS

2   Body Beasts

8   Seeing Tiny Creatures

10   A Closer Look

12   Concept Check

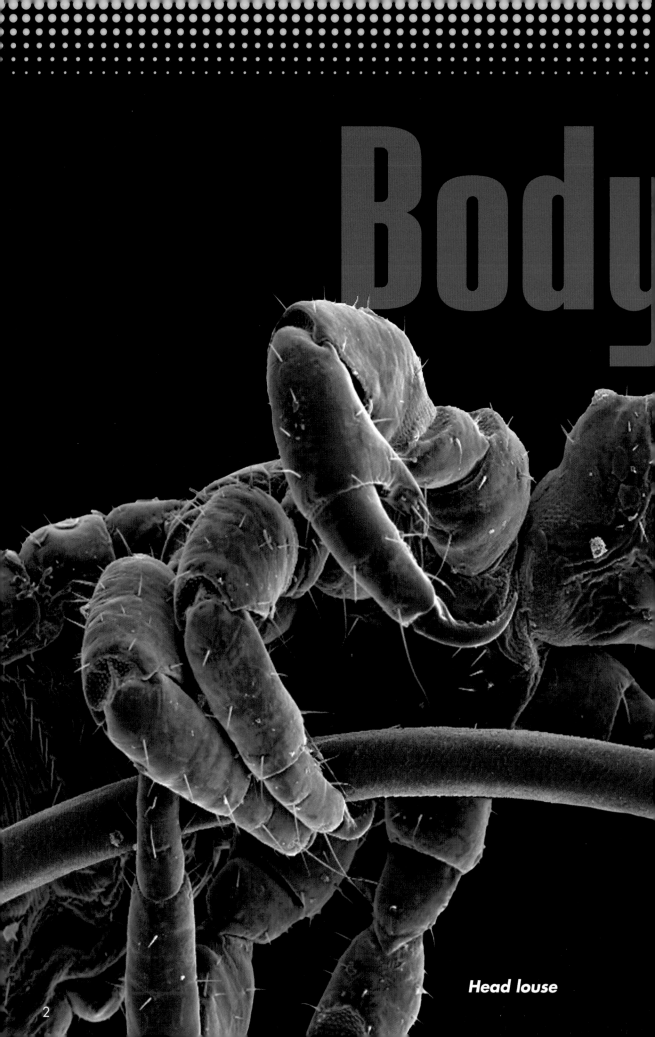

Body

Head louse

Beasts

By Peter Winkler

Animals need places to live.
Some live on other animals.
Some even live on people!
What are these animals like?

Lousy Guests

Lice may be the best known body beasts. They are tiny insects. They live on people. That makes us their **hosts.** A host is an animal or plant that something else lives on.

Lice use their teeth to bite into the host's skin. The bites are too small to hurt. But they can itch.

Thirsty Critters

"Don't let the bedbugs bite!" You may have heard that. Did you ever wonder if bedbugs were real?

They are. Bedbugs are tiny insects. They live in beds, clothes, couches, and chairs. Like lice, bedbugs drink human blood. Their bites can cause skin problems. Itchy bumps can form on your skin.

Ticks are another kind of bug that drinks blood. They cause even more trouble. They carry **germs.** When a tick bites, the germs may get into the host's blood. That can cause sickness.

Hooked on You

Lice, bedbugs, and ticks might seem scary. Yet they are cuddly compared to hookworms.

Hookworms chew right through skin. Then they head to the **intestines.** The intestines are body parts. They are shaped like long tunnels. They turn food into useful chemicals.

Hookworms bite into the intestine walls. They can stay there for years. This causes big problems for the host.

Mites. *These tiny critters could fit on the period ending this sentence. They live at the roots of eyelashes and hairs.*

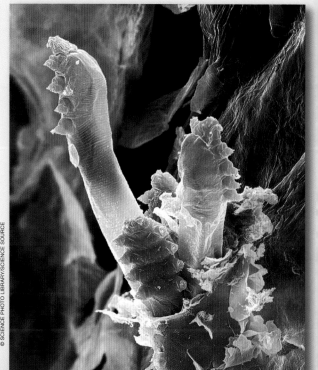

Tick. *This body beast drinks blood. During meals, it swells up like a balloon.*

© DAVID M. PHILIPS/SCIENCE SOURCE

© DAVID SCHARF/GETTY IMAGES

Hookworm. *Hookworms live in sand and soil. They wait to touch an animal or person. Then they eat through the host's skin.*

© KALLISTA IMAGES/GETTY IMAGES

Bedbug. *These animals drink drops of blood while a person sleeps.*

Good Neighbors

By now, you may be grossed out. Fear not. Some body beasts actually help their human hosts.

Take **bacteria.** These are tiny living things. They are neither plants nor animals. Bacteria live just about everywhere. They even live on people.

Helping Inside and Out

People have trillions of bacteria living on or inside them. We are lucky. Bacteria can help in big ways.

Bacteria clean up skin. They eat oil, sweat, and dry skin. They may also fight some germs on skin.

When they eat sweat, bacteria make smelly chemicals. The smell may not seem very nice. Yet it tells you that bacteria are busy cleaning!

Other bacteria live in intestines. These bacteria help people eat. People cannot digest fruits, vegetables, or other food from plants. So bacteria do the job for us.

A Mite Tricky

Body beasts can both help and harm people. For example, dust mites eat dead skin. That helps people. After eating, though, mites create a lot of waste. That can cause some people to get sick.

Many kinds of body beasts make people their home. All these critters live on, in, or near people. That means no one is ever truly alone!

Wordwise

bacteria: tiny living things that are not plants or animals

germ: tiny living thing that can cause sickness

host: plant or animal that is home to a body beast

intestines: tunnel-shaped body parts that turn food into useful chemicals

Human Habitats

The human body is a habitat, or home, for tiny living things. This picture shows where some body beasts live.

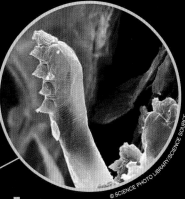

Face Harmless mites live at the roots of eyelashes and other hairs.

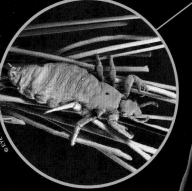

Hair Head lice grip onto hair. They feed by biting the skin and drinking blood.

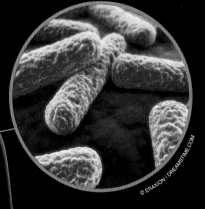

Intestines Bacteria live in these long tunnels. They break down vegetables and grains for us.

Feet Shoes and socks create warm, moist areas. Plant–like growths can cause athlete's foot.

Skin Mosquitoes take blood and can spread disease.

© SCIENCE PHOTO LIBRARY/SCIENCE SOURCE

© EYE

© ERAXION | DREAMSTIME.COM

© BIOPHOTO ASSOCIATION/GETTY IMAGES

© DAVID SCHARF/GETTY IMAGES

© MARK THIESSEN

Seeing

Super Sight. *Scientists use an SEM to look at tiny body beasts.*

S-4100

Tiny Creatures

Most body beasts are tiny. You cannot see them. How do we know what they look like? Machines help us take a closer look. One tool is a scanning electron microscope. It is also called an SEM.

Amazing Pictures

SEMs make things look bigger than they are. They help scientists see very small things, such as body beasts.

To get a picture, scientists first spray metal onto a body beast. This covers it like paint. Then scientists put the beast into the SEM. The SEM scans the metal. It draws a picture of the body beast on a computer screen.

Fabulous Features

SEM pictures let us see the features of body beasts. Some bugs have huge eyes. Some have wings. Some have claws at the end of their legs. Each of these parts helps the bugs survive.

New Tools, New Questions

SEMs have changed the way we look at body beasts. Yet scientists still want to know more. So they ask questions. What body beasts hurt people? What can people do to stay healthy?

New tools help scientists answer their questions. Each day, SEMs and other machines help scientists learn more about body beasts.

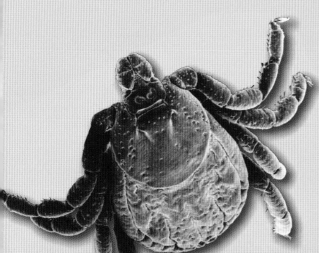

Picture Perfect. *This is a close-up picture of a tick. It was taken by an SEM.*

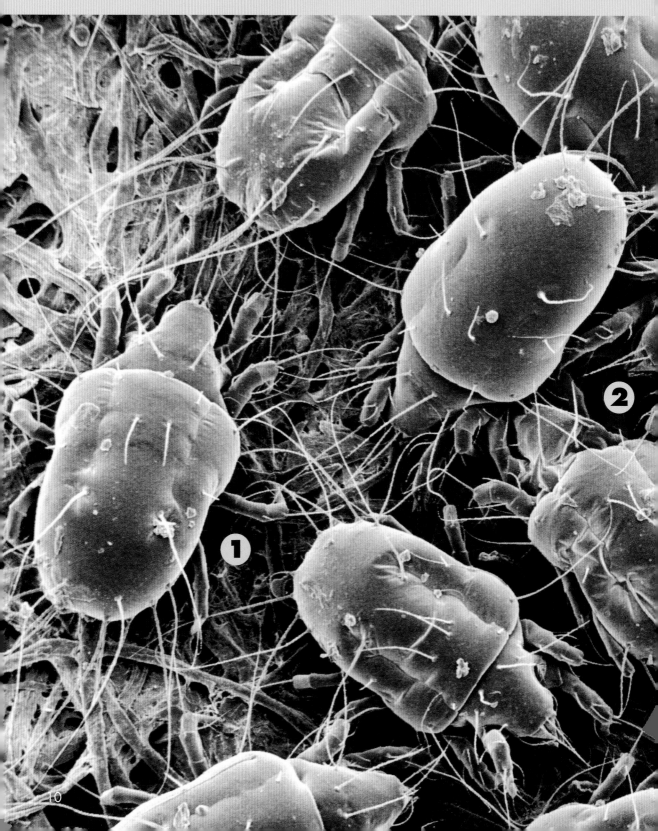

Mites are tiny critters with amazing features. Look at the SEM picture below. What does it show about mites?

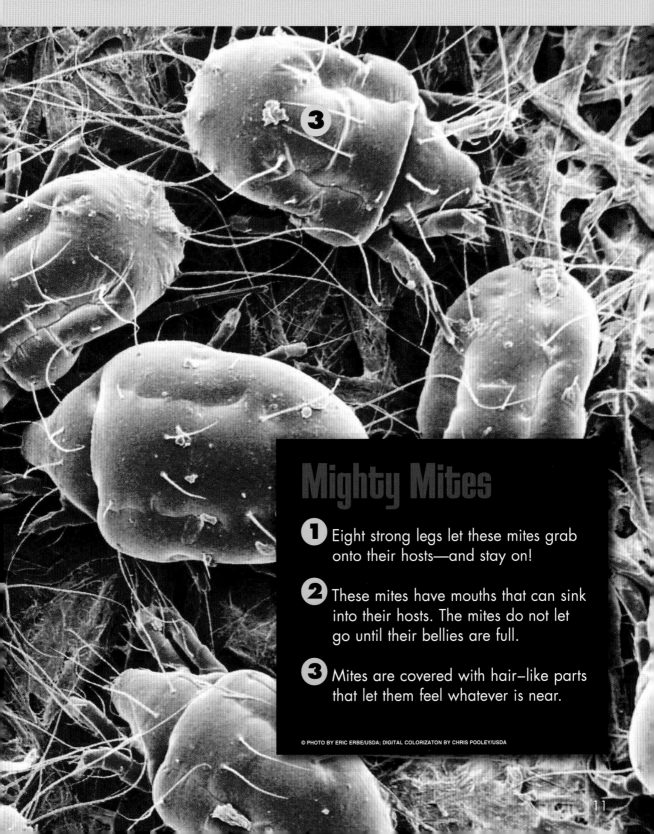

Mighty Mites

1 Eight strong legs let these mites grab onto their hosts—and stay on!

2 These mites have mouths that can sink into their hosts. The mites do not let go until their bellies are full.

3 Mites are covered with hair–like parts that let them feel whatever is near.

© PHOTO BY ERIC ERBE/USDA; DIGITAL COLORIZATON BY CHRIS POOLEY/USDA

Body Beasts

Show what you know about the animals that live on your body.

1 What is a host?

2 Why can some body beasts make people sick?

3 How do bacteria help people?

4 How do SEMs help scientists learn about body beasts?

5 Compare two body beasts. Tell how they are alike. Explain how they are different.